G-PA AND ME

Written and illustrated by

Kelly D. Williams

WestBow Press books may be ordered through booksellers or by contacting:

WestBow Press
A Division of Thomas Nelson & Zondervan
1663 Liberty Drive
Bloomington, IN 47403
www.westbowpress.com
844-714-3454

Interior Image Credit: Kelly D. Williams
Cover Design Credit: Kathryn E. Williams

ISBN: 978-1-6642-6198-3 (sc)
ISBN: 978-1-6642-6197-6 (e)

Library of Congress Control Number: 2022905711

Print information available on the last page.

WestBow Press rev. date: 4/8/2022

WESTBOW
PRESS®
A DIVISION OF THOMAS NELSON
& ZONDERVAN

Dedication:
This book is dedicated to G-Pa, who found joy in the simple things of life. He loved great cars, his cats, and dancing. But most of all, he loved our Gram. His sweet spirit, kind heart, and warm smile made a lasting impression on those who knew him.

G-Pa and Me is dedicated to the memory of Don Gaston (G-Pa) and to those who loved him so well.

Special thanks to Annie, Kady, Kaleb, Charlie, and Bethany for your artistic help, honest critiques, and tireless encouragement. More than that, thank you for loving so completely and selflessly.

His eyes growing dull;
Mine spark with delight.
My dawn just appearing;
He sees evening's light.

1

His hand large and rough,
Mine tiny but tough.
He's big; I'm small.
I'm short; he's tall.

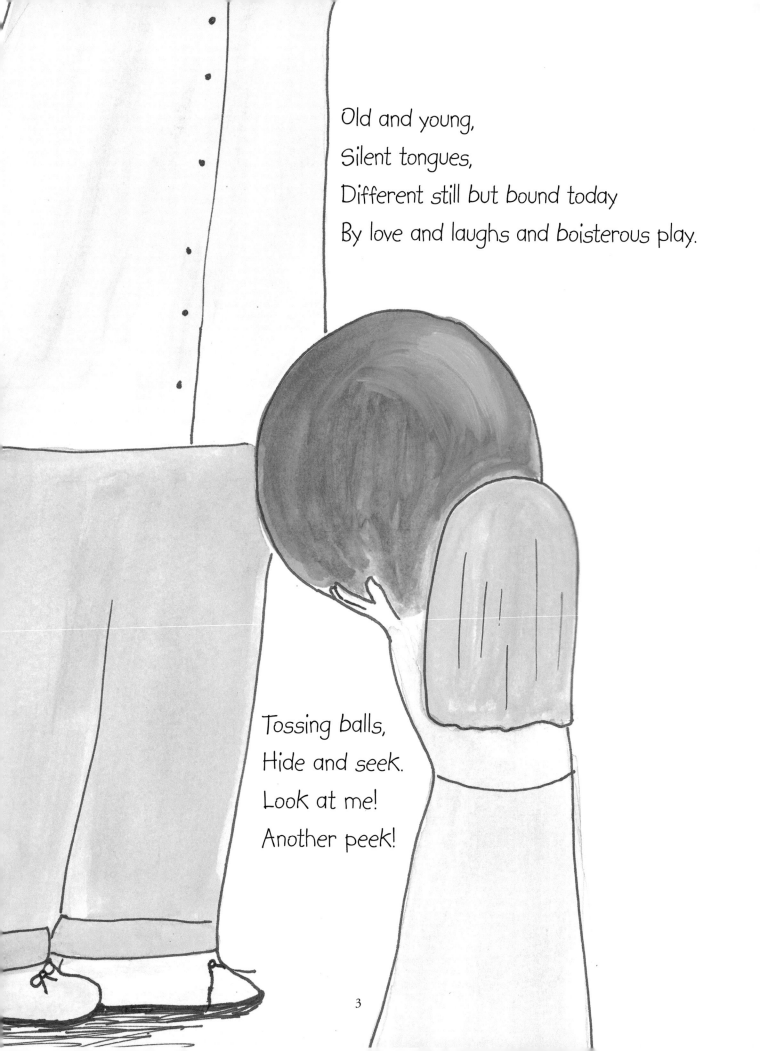

Old and young,
Silent tongues,
Different still but bound today
By love and laughs and boisterous play.

Tossing balls,
Hide and seek.
Look at me!
Another peek!

3

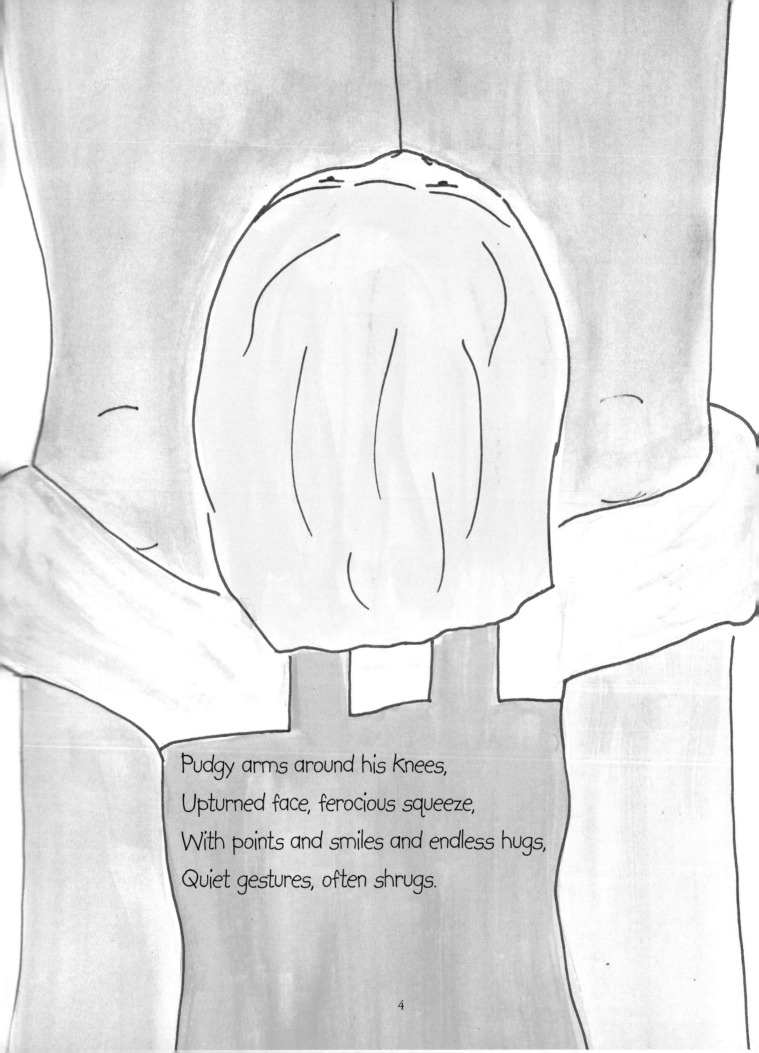

Pudgy arms around his knees,
Upturned face, ferocious squeeze,
With points and smiles and endless hugs,
Quiet gestures, often shrugs.

His words are sometimes hard to find,
Language slipping from his mind,
But love's still there in quiet ways;
The spark is there, but then it fades.

My words are coming faster now;
I'll talk for him and show him how
To play my games and have some fun
In a world seeming darker despite the sun.

Giggles, smiling, shining faces,
Delighted squeals, playing chases,
Never judging or demanding what was,
Only loving what is because...

No expectations but of love,
No worries, trusting God above.
Dimpled cheeks of sweetest peace,
Eyes so full, complete release.

Enjoying what is,
Lingering beauty,
Only joy, not a duty.

Sometimes rules or things forgotten,
Messes made, so much in common!
Adventures with the hairy beasts,
Loving food and having feasts.

Flooding water
Untied shoes
Silly faces
Then a snooze

Today's our day, so we'll have fun!
We'll walk and dance and sometimes run.
Others can't tell what we're thinking,
Mischievous grins, fingers linking.

How do you see the world today?
A place to grow, explore, and play,
Happy with the simple things,
Though days unsure, the joy still rings.

Memories fading, memories building,
A mind that's filled, a mind that's yielding,
Peering through the cobwebbed stare,
Two hearts so loved without a care.

13

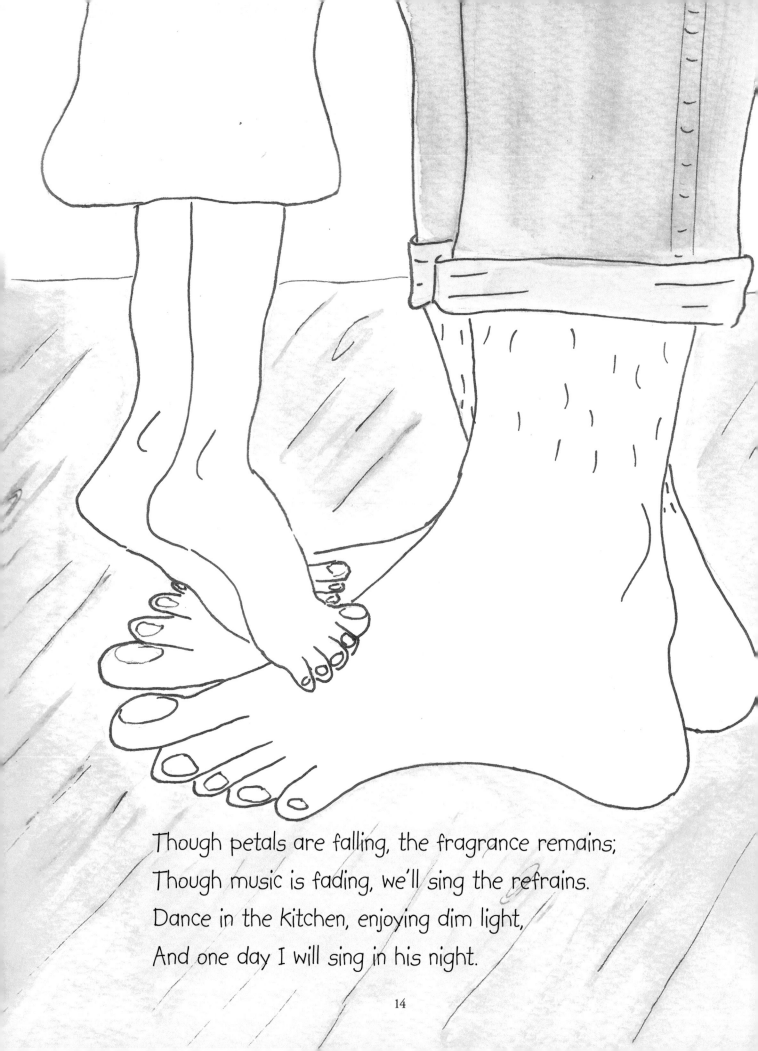

Though petals are falling, the fragrance remains;
Though music is fading, we'll sing the refrains.
Dance in the kitchen, enjoying dim light,
And one day I will sing in his night.

My love will keep growing
and blooming within,
Though his mind will likely
grow dark in the end.

Treasuring each moment
without lament,
Perhaps remembering only
this one moment...

15

Memories unformed but quietly there,
Knowing, feeling acceptance and care;
Impressions wafted and carried on wind,
To a mind far away,
In another place on another day.

Seeds of love planted,
we're quietly tending,
Only protecting,
only giving;

Memories living in the mind of the younger;

The older enjoying the warmth and the hunger.

For him.
Today.
Together.

Tips for Parents:

The effects of dementia touch many families. As you are caring for your loved one and helping your child to cope with the changes occurring in your family, here are some things to keep in mind:

- Don't pretend there aren't changes. Children are very perceptive. Tell them, in age appropriate ways about what is happening in your family.

- If your loved one lives in your home, be sure to carve out some special time each day for your child to spend time talking, playing, or being with you. Keep at least some part of your routine the same (maybe bath time, story time, bedtime). This predictability helps your child to have a sense of security as circumstances around them change.

- Talk about sacrificial love. Remind your child that sometimes doing what is best for others is not easy.

- Children have a huge capacity to love others and spread joy. Encourage them to interact with your loved one. Help them find things they enjoy doing together (swinging on the porch, catching a ball, petting or playing fetch with the dog).

- Talk with your child if they seem afraid or worried. Always remind them that people are precious because they are made in God's image and are loved by Him, no matter what they are physically or mentally able to do.

- Help your child be considerate. If your loved one has a special item, it might not be a good idea for your child to play with that item. This is a great time to talk about respecting the property of others. You can help your child understand by reminding them of a special toy they might not want to share.

- Find ways that your child can help express love. Encourage them to draw pictures, make crafts, communicate via technology, or send cards.

- Don't force your child to show affection in ways they are uncomfortable with. Forcing your child to give hugs and kisses isn't necessary. Encourage your child to find other ways to acknowledge the loved one: high fives, a thumbs up, a wave, or blowing kisses are all great and can be special!

- Make a memory book for your child of the special things he or she does with your loved one. Let your child help you!

Scripture to read with your child:

Leviticus 19:32	Proverbs 20:29	Isaiah 46:4
1 Timothy 5:1-2	Exodus 20:12	Ephesians 6:1-3
Proverbs 23:22	Proverbs 17:6	Deuteronomy 5:16

Others: *(List other Scripture here that you find encouraging. Read it on days when you need extra encouragement.)*

Ideas for Educators:

Antonyms (opposites)
Make a list of antonyms found in the text. How does the author use antonyms to help the reader understand the text? Light/darkness Dawn/evening

Compare/contrast
Create a Venn diagram of the child and the adult in the poem. How are they alike and different?

Figurative Language
Imagery/metaphor- How do the images presented help you to understand the characters mentioned? Phrases such as "Seeds of love planted" help the reader to understand concepts in the text. Make a chart of words or phrases on one side and what concept they are helping the reader to understand on the other side.

Perspective
Who is telling the story? How do you know? How are the perspectives of the two characters different? How do you think each character feels? Make a list of "feeling" words. Older students may use a thesaurus to find new words for their ideas.

Poetry
Identify rhyming words, rhythm and meter, and patterns. Why do you think the author chose to present the story in the form of a poem? How would you have done it? Rewrite a portion of the text as a narrative story.

Connections
Make it personal. Can you make connections?

Text to text: Have you read other texts (fiction or nonfiction) that describe people who have been touched by dementia? How were the texts similar/different? (One of my favorites is *Wilfred Gordon McDonald Partridge* by Mem Fox.)

Text to world: Many people suffer from dementia. What moral dilemma does this bring to society? Do these people still have value? How should those suffering with dementia be treated? Why?

Text to self: Are students reminded of someone when they read the story? Can they feel a deeper empathy for others? Who? How can students be a blessing to someone who has been touched by dementia (maybe a resident in the nursing home or a family member)? What can you do as an individual? A family? A class?

Vocabulary
You might find it helpful to discuss some of these words before reading. Older students might discuss parts of speech, context clues, or multiple meaning words. Feel free to note other words that your class struggles with!

dull	dimple	lament	*Others:*
bound	linger	expectations	
boisterous	duty	shrug	
impressions	mischievous	dim	
pudgy	cobweb	gesture	
ferocious	refrain	upturned	

Printed in the United States
by Baker & Taylor Publisher Services